celebrity photographer

Isabel Thomas

First published in 2015 by Wayland

Copyright © Wayland 2015

All rights reserved
Dewey Number: 770.9'2-dc23
ISBN: 978 0 7502 9458 4
Library ebook ISBN: 978 0 7502 7402 9

10 9 8 7 6 5 4 3 2 1

Concept by Joyce Bentley

Commissioned by Debbie Foy and
Rasha Elsaeed

Produced for Wayland by Calcium
Designer: Paul Myerscough
Editor: Sarah Eason

Printed in China

Wayland is an imprint of
Hachette Children's Group
Part of Hodder & Stoughton
Carmelite House
50 Victoria Embankment
London EC4Y 0DZ

An Hachette UK Company
www.hachette.co.uk

www.hachettechildrens.co.uk

Acknowledgements: Dreamstime: Iofoto 1; Fotolia:
Pavel Losevsky cover bg; Getty Images: 10–11;
Alice Hawkins: 21; Istockphoto: David Ahn 27br;
Adam Lawrence: 4c, 5; Rex Features: Startraks Photo
14–15; Shutterstock: Yuri Arcurs 24–25, Yan B 28–29,
3l, BonD80 27cl, S Bukley 4l, Cinemafestival 27bl,
back cover, EdwinAC 2b, 31tr, Helga Esteb 4r, 13t,
Featureflash 17, Andrew F. Kazmierski 31br, Mike
Ledray 26bl, Left Eyed Photography 30bl, Jim Lopes
30l, Northfoto 22bl, Nagy Melinda 2c, 12, Sergey
Mironov 26tl, Joe Seer 2t, 6–7, Jeff Thrower 27tr,
Pedro Vidal 3br, Vipflash cover; Kim Watson: 8t, 8–9;
Wikipedia: 20th Century Fox 16, Robert Scoble 18.

cover stories

thepeople

theart

thetalk

ADAM LAWRENCE

Radar expert Adam Lawrence specialises in portrait, music and advertising images. He has snapped celebrities and supermodels such as Jason Statham and Alexa Chung.

How old were you when you got your first camera?

I was young, maybe seven or eight years old. My grandfather gave me a camera, and, because of my height, I shot all my grown-up relatives from a low position looking up their nostrils!

How did you get into photography as a career?

When I was 20, I went to college to study Applied Photography, Film and Television. I spent my summer holidays working as a general gofer (assistant) in a fashion photography studio.

When you are not behind the camera, what do you do?

A lot of time is spent retouching photos and getting the images ready for the client. I have to work out quotations, send my invoices and keep my portfolio of work bang up-to-date.

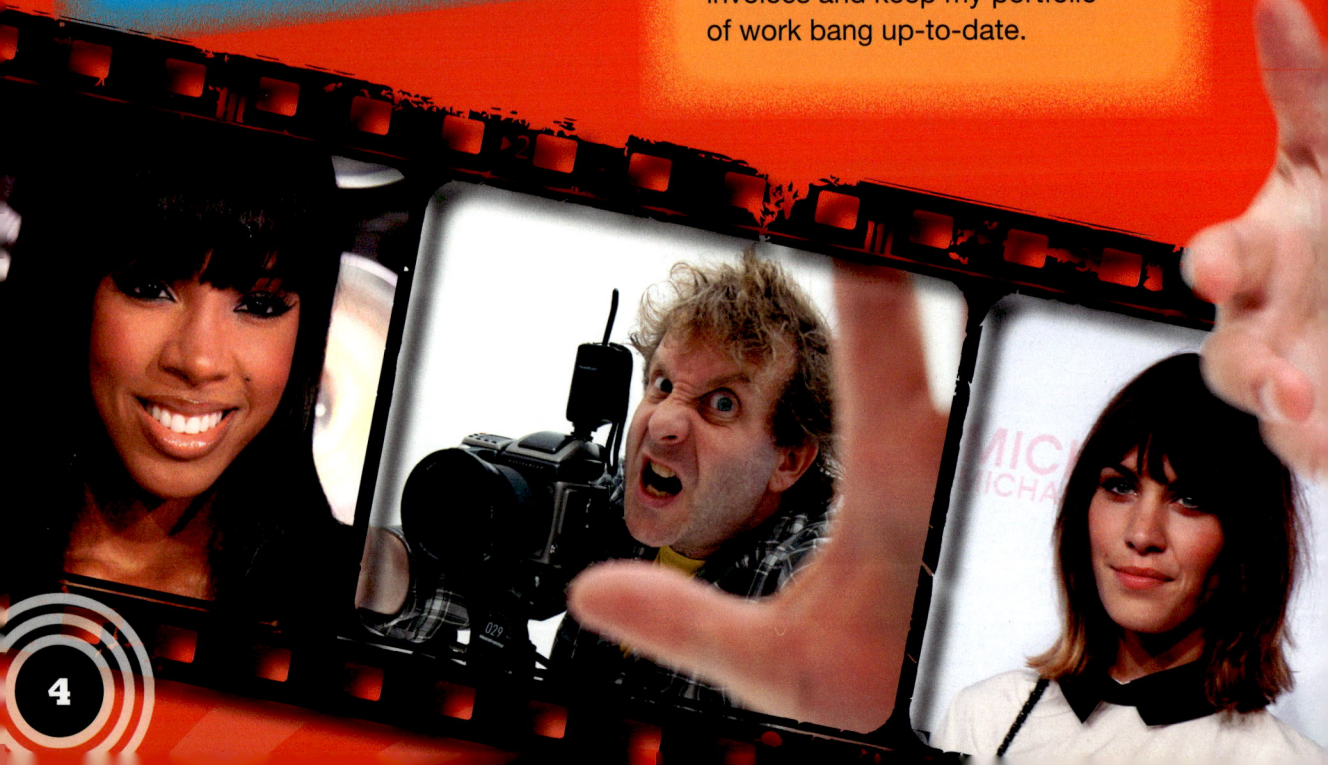

How do you get the best out of celebrity subjects?

Celebrities are used to having their photographs taken and are a lot easier to work with than other people! I always tell them my ideas, and ask if they have any thoughts about the shoot. It's important that they feel relaxed in my company.

What do you do if you have a 'difficult' subject?

I try to make sure that everything is done as quickly and professionally as possible. Once, a supermodel was rude to me in front of a crew of 30 people, so I was rude back! But most of the time I keep cool...

Do you have any top tips?

Know your equipment! I'd say the most important thing of all is to make your clients feel at ease and build up a good rapport with them. The photography stuff comes second to that.

What are the best and worst parts of the job?

The uncertainty about when work is going to come is the hardest part of the job. However, working for myself is also the best part of the job, because I don't have to answer to anyone apart from my clients. I feel very lucky that I love what I do.

Do you have any advice for wannabe photographers?

You can start by taking a photography course at any age. But the most important thing is getting experience by assisting a professional photographer.

Thousands of celebrity images appear in the media every day. They are taken by photographers, who are paid to capture famous faces on camera. There are different kinds of celebrity photographer, from those who are hired for a large daily fee for a photoshoot to those who 'pap' celebrities.

SHOOTING STARS

On the red carpet

Photojournalists are invited to snap celebrities at events such as film premières and parties. The pictures they take are bought by magazines and newspapers. Celebrities pose for the cameras in the hope that a great picture will appear in the press, and so help to promote their films, TV show or books.

Perfect portraits

If celebrities are releasing a book or launching a product, they turn to a portrait photographer. These experts create beautiful photographs that can help to turn stars into icons.

Image control

Celebrity photographers are hired by magazines to take photographs of stars for their interview spreads. The shots are usually taken in a studio or on location. Top photographers are expert in giving image-conscious stars the direction they need during the shoot to create dazzling photographs that make great magazine viewing.

Being 'papped'

Photographers known as paparazzi take un-posed shots, often without permission. They use special equipment and techniques to try and catch A-listers unawares, such as when they are driving or shopping. Some celebrities, such as Justin Bieber (opposite), have fun with the photographers and photograph *them*!

Finding fame

Successful celebrity portrait photographers are famous artists in their own right. They produce books and exhibitions of their work. Among the best are Annie Leibovitz, Mario Testino, Rankin and David Bailey.

On a shoot with top photographer

KIM WATSON

FRIDAY MARCH 2, 2012

6am I get up nice and early for the shoot. This gives me time to check my gear. I normally pack my cameras, computer, cables, cards and other equipment the night before, but it's always worth double-checking.

8am I arrive at the studio 30 minutes before the call time and meet my two assistants. I'm shooting the latest bridal and couture ranges by designer Bruce Oldfield. When the hair and make-up artists and the model Masha (in the photograph right) arrive, we eat breakfast.

9.30am We all sit down to discuss the looks and shots that we're after. As Masha starts two hours of hair and make-up, my assistants set up the lights. Our first job is to black out the studio as we need carefully controlled lighting. We're shooting against a white background, which should be straightforward, but I have to make sure we have enough definition between the white dress and background.

11.30am Masha walks on set: her whole look is breathtaking. There is always a feeling of excitement when a shoot first starts. I also feel nervous as I want everything to go smoothly.

1pm Lunch was planned for 1pm, but we crack on to get all the bridalwear done before we break. Masha is a joy to work with and we both get into a rhythm.

2pm After a fantastic morning's shoot we break for lunch.

3pm After lunch, we turn our attention to the couture. We're shooting against grey and the look is more moody. My assistants change the lighting set while hair and make-up work their magic to create a bolder look. Our wrap time is supposed to be 6pm, so we all work hard to finish the shoot by then.

5.45pm 'It's a wrap!' I shout. I thank everyone for their hard work. As a surprise, the client has ordered some champagne for us and thanks us all for making the shoot a success.

6pm While my assistants pack up everything, I sit down with the art director and we go over the day's shots. We make a quick edit, to get everyone's instant reactions.

9pm By this point I'm exhausted, and I like to get home and relax. I have a couple of weeks to work on improving the photographs before sending them to the client. Once I've chosen the best shots, I'll send them to an expert retoucher to make my changes. At the same time, I'll ask the art director for his feedback to make sure that he is happy with the photographs before we finally show them to the client. Then, it's fingers crossed that he loves the shots as much as we do!

MAKING DREAMS

Celebrity photographers don't always aim to capture reality. In this shoot, Annie Leibovitz transformed US singer Queen Latifah into a Disney character.

Annie takes dozens of shots, so that she can choose the best one to create the final picture. She says that when she is working with talented actors, incredible images can be captured in just a few minutes.

Type 'celebs get Disney make-over – ABC news' into www.google.com to see the finished photograph and other pieces.

A wind machine is used to move Queen Latifah's wig. It gives the final photos an active look, bringing the character to life.

Annie's assistants help to position the lighting props, to get the right effect. This umbrella can be moved to diffuse light exactly where Annie needs it.

Queen Latifah strikes a pose to capture the spirit of Ursula, the evil sea witch in the Disney film *The Little Mermaid*. The final image was used in Disney's 'Dream Portraits' advertising campaign, which featured three pictures of celebrities dressed as Disney heroes and villains.

Elaborate costumes help each photo to tell a story. The amazing octopus costume was built and arranged by costume designers and technicians before the shoot, so that Queen Latifah just had to wriggle into it.

Ursula lives in the ocean, but Annie shot the pictures in a studio so the lighting could be carefully controlled. A dark background represents the colours of the ocean depths. After the shoot, computer software is used to add a stormy sky and crashing waves, so Ursula appears to be in the sea.

Before

After

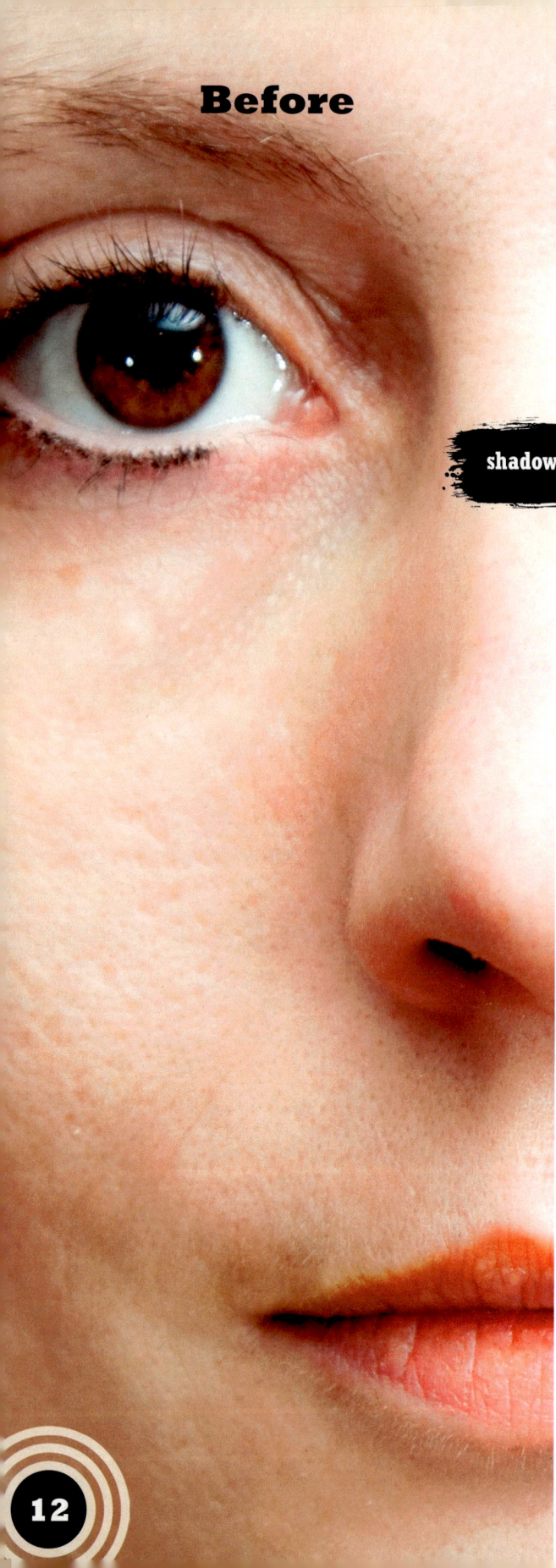

shadows removed

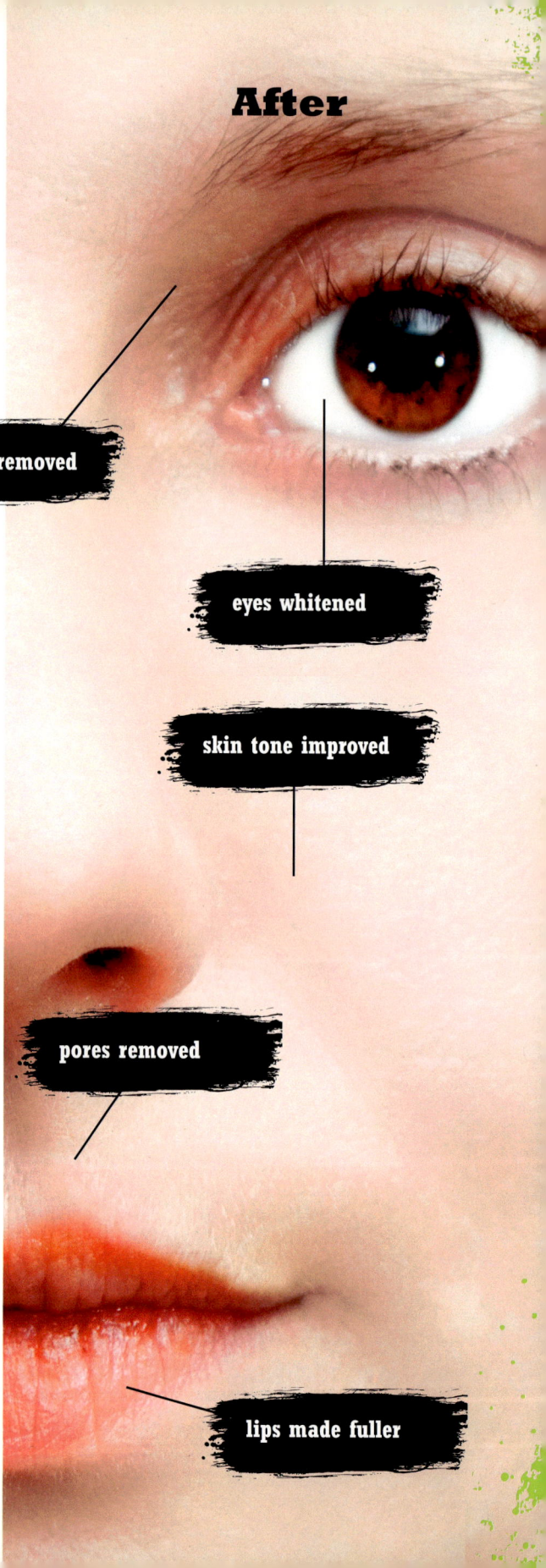

eyes whitened

skin tone improved

pores removed

lips made fuller

PICTURE PERFECT?

One of the most controversial aspects of modern celebrity photography is the editing of digital images to erase errors such as blemishes and eyebags. Known as 'retouching', in some cases the technique is even used to alter a celebrity's body shape. Could these 'perfect' images be harming our health?

Can images of celebrities such as Miley Cyrus (right) have a negative effect on us?

now so advanced that most photographs present images of 'perfect' people and readers rarely get to see reality at all. Many believe that celebrities look as good in real life as they do in their photographs.

Faking it

In just one issue of the magazine US *Vogue*, 107 advertisements, 36 fashion pictures and the cover image were retouched. The aim of retouching is to create pictures that people like to look at. Standard retouching techniques include sharpening images to make them look clearer and improving the colour quality. But they also include changing aspects of people's faces and bodies. This results in photographs that show 'perfect' people.

Nothing new

Photographers argue that retouching is nothing new. Before computers were invented, flattering lighting, wide-angled lenses and darkroom tricks were used to make stars look better in stills. The problem today is that retouching skills are

Health warnings

Scientists have found that retouched images of celebrities can make people feel bad about their own bodies. In the UK, France and the USA, campaigners have called for the labelling of these images, so people know they are not real.

Some celebrities are speaking out to reassure their fans. US star Miley Cyrus wrote in her autobiography, 'I'd see…photoshopped images of myself in magazines, and see this perfect, airbrushed version of myself. Then I'd look in the mirror and see reality…If you ever find yourself wishing you looked as good as Miley Cyrus in some photo…just remember: *Miley Cyrus* doesn't look as good as Miley Cyrus in that photo!'.

HELENA CHRISTENSEN

Model start

Helena is half Peruvian, but grew up in Copenhagen and began modelling when she was nine years old. At 18, she was crowned Miss Denmark. Helena wanted to be a photographer, and she thought modelling would be a good way to travel the world taking photos. She moved to Paris, France, and then became one of the most famous supermodels of the 1980s and 1990s.

THE STATS

Name: Helena Christensen
Date of birth: 25 December 1968
Lives: Copenhagen, Denmark, and New York City, USA
Nationality: Danish
Job: Photographer, model and boutique owner

Shooting celebrities

In the 1990s, Helena used her contacts in fashion magazines, and started to take on paid photography work. She shot magazine photographs and portraits of pop stars, actors and fellow models. Her experience as a model helped Helena to get the best out of her subjects. In 1999, she helped to launch the fashion magazine *Nylon*, shooting film star Liv Tyler for the cover.

Stepping behind the lens

For 15 years, Helena took her camera everywhere she went, building a large collection of beautiful pictures. Modelling for some of the world's leading fashion photographers taught her new tricks. She says that her modelling career gave her the perfect education to be a photographer. By watching expert photographers at work, she picked up their techniques and methods.

Going solo

When Helena was 35, the first exhibition of her photography was held in London. Since then, her work has been shown in Amsterdam in the Netherlands and New York, USA, and has been published in the world's top magazines. Today, Helena still models, but photography is her number-one interest. She often shoots celebrity images for charity projects and has travelled to Nepal and Peru to take pictures for charity. She loves her new role as a photographer and says, 'When you work behind the lens, you don't have to consider any limits.'

STAR MAKERS

The public's appetite for celebrity photographs began soon after cameras were invented. Since then, pictures have become an essential part of every star's career.

Before the age of the paparazzi, photographs of film stars such as the legendary 1940s actress Rita Hayworth were taken only by professional photographers in studios.

Celebrity culture

In the 1920s and 1930s, magazines such as *Life* were launched. They were filled with photographs of the famous and infamous. Hollywood film studios used glamorous portraits to promote new films, turning actors such as Rita Hayworth and Clark Gable into stars.

Fame sells

Early photographers used celebrity photos to attract new customers into their studios. In the nineteenth century, American photographer Mathew Brady displayed pictures of famous people in his studio windows. People flocked to see the photographs, buy prints and have their own portraits taken. Brady published the first book of celebrity portraits in 1850.

Snapping secrets

In the 1960s, photojournalists began focusing on celebrities' private lives. They became known as 'paparazzi', after a photographer in the film *La Dolce Vita* (1960), who chases a journalist across Rome to catch him misbehaving. Paparazzi photographers have captured many newsworthy moments, but they have also been criticised for the techniques they use to capture outrageous pictures of stars. These include using long lenses, or posing as decorators to get into a celebrity's house.

A growing demand

The second half of the twentieth century saw an explosion in the number of magazines, newspapers and TV channels. The rise of the internet added to the number of ways people could access celebrity images. By the end of the century, celebrity photos were in high demand. Top celebrity photographers, such as Mario Testino, became as famous as the stars that posed for them.

With the explosion of celebrity culture in the 1990s, photographers such as Mario Testino became celebrities in their own right.

All change

Today, many stars only agree to be photographed when they have something to promote, such as a film, album or perfume. Paparazzi photographers fill in the gaps. However, there is a new type of celebrity photographer. High-quality digital and mobile phone cameras mean that fans can take photographs and upload them in seconds. In the twenty-first century, it has become more and more popular to snap celebrities, and as a result the income of paparazzi photographers may fall...

ANNIE LEIBOVITZ

Living legend

THE STATS

Date of birth:
2 October 1949
Born: Connecticut, USA
Lives: New York City, USA
Job: Freelance photographer

Leibovitz says of celebrities 'I am more interested in what they do than what they are.' Her attitude and talent have made her one of the most popular celebrity photographers ever.

Discovering photography

While Annie was at college in the late 1960s, she took a trip to Japan and discovered that she loved taking photographs. She began taking evening classes to learn camera skills. In 1970, she sent some of her photographs to the American magazine *Rolling Stone*. The editor was impressed, and commissioned Annie to photograph one of the biggest popstars of all time – *The Beatles* lead signer, John Lennon.

Radical rock images

Annie's first shoot appeared on the magazine's cover in 1971. She began working as a freelance photographer, and became *Rolling Stone's* chief photographer in 1973. Annie worked for the magazine for ten years, shooting hundreds of pictures of music stars, including an amazing 142 covers!

Celebrity glamour

In 1983, Annie joined the staff of *Vanity Fair* magazine, where she became famous for her glamorous celebrity portraits. Rather than natural-looking shots, she prefers to take photographs using props and lighting to create striking scenes. She also persuades her subjects to do unusual or outrageous things. Her famous *Vanity Fair* images include actress Whoopi Goldberg lying in a bath of milk and actress Kate Winslet floating underwater. One of Annie's most talked about shots is of Miley Cyrus wearing nothing but a bedsheet.

Career highlights

1983 published her first book of photographs, *Annie Leibovitz: Photographs*

1984 won the American Society of Magazine Photographers Photographer of the Year Award

1987 won Campaign of the Decade Award from *Advertising Age* magazine, for her American Express Portraits campaign

1990 won the Infinity Award for Applied Photography from the International Center of Photography, New York, USA

1998 begins work for US *Vogue*

2000 awarded a Living Legend Award by the US Government

Fame and fortune

Annie became the photographer of choice for the world's most famous and powerful figures. Her pictures also won her big advertising clients, who paid her up to US$100,000 a day to create magical images. Today, Annie combines magazine and advertising work, and a team of up to 30 assistants and stylists help her on every shoot. Her photographs have been exhibited at museums and galleries around the world, and have made Annie as famous as the many people she photographs. She is considered the most successful photographer in history.

THE DREAM JOB

My story by Alice Hawkins

I was 14 when I decided to take a GCSE in photography and got my first SLR film camera. I went on to study graphic design at university, and after just a day's work experience with a professional photographer, I realised what a wonderful job it could be!

My big break came when someone from the top style magazine *i-D* saw my work displayed at my end-of-degree show. He called me the next day and asked if I'd like to start shooting for the magazine. The following week, I was photographing celebrities at fashion parties in London! It was such a thrill to see my pictures published in an iconic magazine.

Since then, I've been commissioned to photograph dozens of celebrities including Gisele Bündchen, Kanye West, Jessie J, Girls Aloud and Beth Ditto. One of my best memories is photographing Elvis Presley's granddaughter Riley on a Californian mountain ranch with a horse. I just couldn't get over the fact her grandad was Elvis – it was amazing!

When I get a great shot, I feel really happy and exhausted at the same time. I'm often running on adrenalin, and staying up until the early hours of the morning looking through my pictures. Editing can be the hardest part of the job.

The best part of my job is photographing strangers from all walks of life, and getting the best picture I possibly can. Everyone I photograph is a celebrity or supermodel to me, and sometimes we become great friends! I also enjoy travelling, making memories and the freedom to be nosey in people's homes – great perks of the job!

My dream is to photograph Dolly Parton. I adore her music and I adore her. I've been trying for years. I'm not going to give up!

SHOOT SPEAK

Pocket some 'pap' speak with our lingo guide!

cast
the people who appear in a TV show, film, play, music video or group photograph

crew
the people who work behind the scenes on a TV show, film, play, music video or photoshoot

gofer
a person who acts as an assistant and runs simple errands

celebrity
a famous person, such as a pop star, actor or actress, member of the royalty or a politician

diffuse
to spread something out across a wide area; diffused light is not concentrated on one area, so it is soft

lens hood
a shade around a camera lens, used to stop light entering the lens from the side, to improve picture quality

flash
short for 'flash gun'. A flash is a short burst of very bright light from a camera and is used to brighten the subject

light meter
a device used to tell the photographer how dark or light a subject is. The photographer uses it to set up their camera and flash correctly

freelance
when someone is self-employed and works for different companies on short-term contracts

long lens
another word for 'telephoto lens'. A lens on a camera that allows the photographer to zoom in from a long distance

Paparazzi often take images of famous people without their permission, but the stars can request that the faces of their children are blurred if the image is published.

paparazzi (pap)
a photographer who takes unposed pictures of celebrities, often without their permission

photojournalist
a photographer who takes pictures to illustrate news stories

Photoshop
computer software that is used to edit digital photographs

portfolio
a collection of creative work, such as photographs, that are used to win new work. Portfolios are provided digitally today, such as on a website or a CD

portrait
a photograph, painting or drawing of a person

reflector
a white surface that reflects light back onto the subject

retouching
altering an image using computer software such as Photoshop; also known as airbrushing

roll (for backgrounds)
coloured or white rolls of fabric or paper used as a backdrop behind the subject during a photoshoot

SLR
stands for single-lens reflex: a type of camera that allows photographers to see exactly what they are about to shoot when they look through the viewfinder

soft box
a box-shaped piece of fabric that is placed around a photographic light to diffuse the light and make it softer

still
an ordinary photograph, or single image, taken from a series of images, which makes up a cinema film

telephoto lens
see 'long lens'

umbrella
an umbrella-shaped device that reflects light

zoom
to focus in on a subject to take a detailed shot

GLOSSARY

A-lister
a very famous person

adrenalin
a hormone found in the human body that causes the heart to beat faster and gives a 'rushing' feeling

infamous
well-known for something bad

press
newspapers and other print media

rapport
a close relationship in which the people understand each other's feelings or ideas and communicate well

IN THE FRAME

The lighting is set up and the music on. The A-list actor strolls in and I introduce myself. He is one of the biggest stars I've worked with to date, so the pressure is on to make sure the shoot goes well. I have just one hour to capture the shot before he is whisked off to the next stop in his packed schedule. It's all systems go!

Open up

I've heard that he hates having his picture taken, so I'm going to have to work hard to get him to relax in front of the camera. I make a few jokes and he laughs. I can tell that he looks more at ease, so I suggest we start taking some shots. I put on some music as I prepare my camera and other equipment – it always helps to keep the mood relaxed. Then, I get to work taking the all-important photos.

Capture it

The photos I've taken are good, but I know they could be even better. I want to change the mood of the shoot, so I talk to the actor to explain my thinking. It's no good barking instructions like a drill sergeant at a top celebrity! If you can get them to see your vision and work with you, it's the best way to capture a picture that everyone will remember.

Break the ice

Every few seconds, I glance at my digital display, checking the images as I take them. I tell him that he doesn't look his best in the shots and I think we need to call in the stylists. He's shocked, but then breaks into a huge grin. Famous people aren't used to being criticised, but I get the feeling this star prefers honesty. The stylists touch up his hair, and we're back on track.

The perfect moment

We enter the last few minutes of the shoot. Finally, my subject truly drops his guard, and relaxes. Perfect. I adjust the lighting to match the mood in the studio. The ideal shots start to come, and I know I've hit the jackpot. For a few minutes we're working together and he poses for the shots like a trained professional model. When he leaves the room, I'm buzzing with adrenalin. I've got hours of editing ahead, working into the night, and a tough deadline to meet, but I know it will be worth it.

LIGHT WORK

After the camera, light is a celebrity photographer's most important tool. Special equipment is used to control the way light falls on a subject, from erasing hard shadows to creating the effect of sunlight in a studio.

A soft box is fixed around a light to diffuse the light and make it less harsh.

Styling shadows

The main light controls the angle of the shadows on the subject's face. Getting the shadows in the right place is important to emphasise a celebrity's best features. Dark shadows create a dramatic image. A 'fill' light, set up in a different position, can be used to lighten shadows and make the image look softer and prettier.

Flattering faces

Bare bulbs give out a harsh light, which may be perfect for a mean and moody look. When glamour is the aim, soft boxes and reflector umbrellas are used to soften the light. These tools diffuse light, by bouncing it off a larger surface, or passing it through thin fabric. This gives shadows a softer edge.

Background lighting

A good celebrity photograph draws the eye to its star subject, but that doesn't mean the photographer can forget about the background. This changes the mood of a photograph, making the image look more interesting. In the studio, photographers hang up large sheets of paper, muslin cloth or velvet, for a smooth, seamless look. White or black are the most popular colours for portraits. These simple backgrounds can be lit up in many ways to produce hundreds of different effects.

A lens hood stops light hitting the lens from the side, making colours look richer.

Reflector umbrellas and white backdrops help to reflect light.

Modern flash units can be tilted to direct the light towards a reflective surface.

A light meter measures the amount of light falling on a subject and helps the photographer decide which camera settings to use.

A laptop computer allows photographers to view their shots instantly, and see if the lighting needs adjusting.

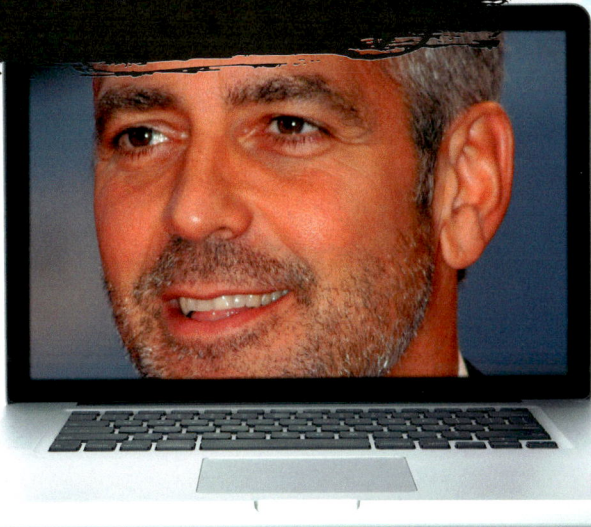

SNAPPY STATS

£160

The average amount paid for a paparazzi shot of an A-list celebrity.

£9 MILLION

The fee paid by *Hello!* magazine for the first photos of Brad Pitt and Angelina Jolie's twins.

£1 MILLION

The fee paid in 1999 by *OK!* magazine for David and Victoria Beckham's wedding pictures. It was one of the magazine's best-selling issues ever.

500,000

The number of copies of *People* magazine sold when it published the exclusive first photo of Shiloh Jolie-Pitt. 800,000 more copies than usual were bought!

£158 THOUSAND

The average amount of money earned each year by top celebrity photographers such as Mario Testino and Rankin.

£1.2 MILLION

The amount of money paid to celebrity photographer Annie Leibovitz in 2009 for her work for the magazine *Vanity Fair*.

14 YEARS

The age of the world's youngest paparazzi photographer, Austin Visschedyk, when he started snapping Hollywood celebrities.

£25 THOUSAND

The yearly salary earned by average celebrity photographers.

BAN THE PAPS?

FOR

Critics say that everyone has a right to privacy, and that paparazzi photographs can be harmful. They say:

1. When celebrities are 'off-duty' they have a right to a private life. A celebrity's personal relationships can be harmed by constant stalking by photographers.

2. Some paparazzi chase celebrities to find out where they are going. This infringement of privacy can be both dangerous and threatening. In 1997, Diana, Princess of Wales, was killed in a car crash while being chased by photographers in France. Since then, France and California, USA, have introduced anti-paparazzi laws.

3. It's not just the celebrities who are affected by the paparazzi. Their families are often harassed by photographers, too. Many relatives of celebrities never sought fame, yet their personal lives have also been invaded by the press.

4. Illegal tactics have been used by paparazzi to get photographs. These include jumping red lights and setting off fire alarms to make celebrities exit a building. Photographers will also trespass on a celebrity's property, crash into a celebrity's car on purpose and pose as family members to get into a hospital. By publishing these photographs, magazines are encouraging criminal behaviour.

AGAINST

Other people argue that paparazzi are not the problem. They are only providing the pictures that the public want to see. They say:

1. Many magazines, newspapers and websites depend on celebrity pictures. If there were no paparazzi pictures, a huge industry would be affected.
2. The public will always want to know about their favourite stars. Celebrities rely on media photos and interviews to get work and should accept that people want to see pictures of them.
3. Taking a photograph is harmless as long as the paparazzi do not break laws.
4. Freedom of the press is very important. Some people are worried that making laws against photographing famous faces may threaten that freedom. Newspapers and magazines are not just about celebrity gossip. People rely on the press to find out important things about our world and the people who run it.
5. Paparazzi photographs show celebrities' flaws as well as their good points. They are important because they show that the retouched publicity shots of stars are not 'real'.

RIGHT OR WRONG?

Paparazzi take pictures that the public want to see, and demand for pictures is fuelled by stars trying to remain in the public eye. However, people who enjoy looking at pictures may be shocked by the tactics sometimes used to take them. The media need to work with paparazzi to make sure that taking photographs does not harm the subjects of the pictures.

SHOOT THIS!

Want to find out more about being a celebrity photographer? Use the Radar guide to put yourself in the frame for this fantastic career!

People to talk to

The Royal Photographic Society
Anyone can contact or become a member of the Royal Photographic Society, both amateurs and professionals. Check out the galleries in their learning zone:
www.rps.org

Victoria and Albert Museum, London
The V&A website is packed with information on photography as art, including a mini-site dedicated to photojournalism:
www.vam.ac.uk

Places to visit

National Portrait Gallery, London
Be inspired by the very best portrait photography:
www.npg.org.uk

Reads & Apps

The Digital Photography Handbook by Doug Harman (Quercus Publishing, 2010)

The Quick Expert's Guide to Mobile Phone Photography by Janet Hoggarth (Wayland, 2012)

Adobe Photoshop Express
Professional photo editing software can be expensive, but you can get a brilliant taster with the free *Adobe Photoshop Express* app. Download it from:
www.itunes.com
https://market.android.com

INDEX